YOGA
THE SPIRIT OF UNION

Third Edition

Lar Caughlan

with postures demonstrated by
Yogi Marthandan and Suzanne Stevenot

KENDALL/HUNT PUBLISHING COMPANY
4050 Westmark Drive   Dubuque, Iowa   52002

CONTENTS

Foreword, **v**
Preface, **vii**
Introduction, **ix**

Chapter One—Sun Salutations, **2**
    The Sun Salutations, **4**

Chapter Two—Beginning Postures, **14**
    The Cobra, **16**
    The Locust, **18**
    The Bow, **20**
    The Forward Bend, **22**
    The Wheel, **24**
    The Shoulder Stand and the
       Fish, **26**
    The Spinal Twist, **28**
    The Triangle, **30**
    The Tree, **34**
    The Diamond, **36**
    The Corpse Pose—Deep
       Relaxation, **39**

Chapter Three—Advanced Variations, **40**
    The Headstand, **42**
    Inverted Tree, **44**
    The Scorpion from Elbow
       Stand, **46**
    Horus the Falcon Overlooking
       the Crow in the Lotus, **48**
    The Unilateral Foot Hand
       Posture, **50**

The Peacock, **52**
The Pigeon, **54**
The Full Bow, **56**
The Wheel—Extensions, **58**
The Scorpion, on the Hands, **60**
Strength and Courage—The King
    Dancer, **64**
Leg to the Head, **66**
The Yoga Sleep, **68**
Five Birds Roof Perching, **70**
The Rabbit, **72**

Gurus, **79**
Wheel with Moon Bridge, **82**
Leg Lunge from Scorpion on the
    Elbows, **84**
Appendix I Attention and Caution, **85**
Appendix II Headstand Lunge, **86**
Appendix III, Headstand Leg Lunge, **87**
Appendix IV Lunge from Elbow
    Scorpion, **88**
Appendix V, **89**
Appendix VI Handstand Lunge
    Progression, **90**
Appendix VII, **91**
Appendix VIII Bibliography, **92**
Appendix IX, **94**
Appendix X, **95**

Swami Satchidananda

Summer Residence.
Yogaville
Box 108, Pomfret Center
Connecticut 06259, USA
Phone: (203) 974-1005

Swami *Satchidananda*

Winter Residence:
La Paz
2336 Bella Vista Drive
Santa Barbara
California 93108, USA
Phone: (805) 969-1363

FOREWORD

Hatha Yoga is no longer a science only for the Himalayan cave dwellers. Millions of people all over the globe are practicing this science with remarkable benefits. Hatha Yoga bestows health, vitality and ease to the physical, vital and mental bodies of the practitioner.

Lawrence Caughlan's Yoga poses proclaim the powerful and sculptural qualities of the body, coupled with the dynamic beauty of nature. These photographs do not require any lengthy explanation. Mr. Caughlan has clearly demonstrated that 'a picture is worth a thousand words'.

I feel that this book will create a deep interest in the minds of its readers, encouraging them to become more involved in this great science of Yoga. After all, the fact is that everyone would like to have an easeful body, peaceful mind and a useful life which is the goal of Yoga however it is presented.

May I wish the author and the readers as well, all the health, peace and joy that is truly our birthright.

Ever Yours in Yoga,

Swami Satchidananda

Buckingham , Virginia 2 April 1981

The dedicated ever enjoy Supreme Peace. Therefore, live only to serve.

"It is an excellent thing to attain this vision of union in diversity, to feel others live in ourselves and to perceive ourselves living in others.

Thus myself and yourself have lived in interdependence. . . ."

Quote from "Initiations and Initiates in Tibet" by Alexandria David-Neel 1867–1969

PREFACE

I began the photography for this book twenty two years ago and if, as they say, "A picture is worth a thousand words," then these pictures have saved me a lot of writing. Whatever the case, I wrote the text in fourteen days—brevity, my prevailing discipline.

I am grateful for the many hearty friends who helped me shoot these photographs. Often there were long treks through genuine wilderness, with precarious environments at the end. My final request before assuming each pose was always, "Make sure to catch a shot in mid-air if I fall!" I'm glad I won't need to say that anymore!

In order of their photographic contribution: Fairlie Page Shanner, Suzanne Stevenot, Lar Caughlan, Mike Mc-Guire, Bill Bonebrake, Veron Dunn, John Dewood and Linda Andersen.

I chose two distinct environments for writing the text: a Wilderness 21' sailboat named "Silver Gael" and various train yards throughout the state of California. The first location is self explanatory; the second, perhaps not.

There's something about the rhythm, flux and flow, and occasional dynamic presence at a train yard, spelled by long intervals of silence, that I found conducive to introspection and easy withdrawal from my memory bank. (See poem for the Locust pose.)

I am grateful to Sri Swami Satchidananda for his wonderful inspiration in my life and for his warm generous foreword.

To my mother Jeanne who taught me to constructively savor my freedom, to my Brother Rob who always busted me whenever I got "Holier than thou", to my friend Brian Rohan who taught me of "Celtic generosity", and to Martha Miller for her aid and manual dexterity.

Also to Ron Croci who taught me to see with the eye of a photographer; to Dave and Phil Bircheff, two Gurus of technical rock climbing; to Siva Fiske, for his inspiration as a brother yogi. And Rick Nelson who got me to hear Swami Chinmayananda, 1963.

I searched through "The Ages" to locate the inspirational quotes which accompany the photographs. Each is uniquely linked to the theme of the book, The Spirit of Union.

"Hanging Five" Pedro Point, 1963

INTRODUCTION

In Hindu mythology, Marthanda was the eighth egg laid by the great sky eagle, Garuda. The first seven eggs hatched into saints and the eighth, Marthanda, into the Sun.

On January 20, 1972, I received the Yoga name Marthandan from my guru, Sri Swami Satchidananda. Within two weeks my new name took on a dynamic significance when I received a position at the San Francisco zoo teaching eagles how to fly and be free.

It was six years earlier, on the day I climbed my first ascent of the High Sierra Nevada Mountains, the 10,850 foot Mount Hoffman, that I began my serious practice of Yoga. My legs were dog-tired when I finally returned with my climbing partner, Mal Hall, to our base camp. I instinctively flipped up into the shoulder stand and instantly gained the firsthand experience of the benefits of Hatha Yoga. Even before this, in my youth as an avid "surf bum" I learned to fuse with nature through the rhythmic flowing, rolling meditations called surfing and skin diving.

I spent the following years exploring the combined disciplines of mountaineering and Yoga, finding total compatibility. I studied numerous Hatha Yoga techniques and read all the books I could find. I went to lectures of Swamis, Roshis, Priests and Shamans, searching for a

Summit—Mount Hoffman, 1966

master from whom I could study more seriously. Finally I heard a talk by Swami Satchidananda. Immediately I joined the Integral Yoga Institute of which he is the founder and director.

In time I graduated from the Teacher training course and began teaching free classes at San Francisco State University where I had been majoring in music and film.

The campus in the late sixties and early seventies was in great turmoil because of the Vietnam "Conflict" and students and faculty together would come in off the picket lines to "mellow out" in the Yoga class. Inspired by the writings of Gandhi and Martin Luther King, I too became involved in the non-violent protest and the Civil Rights Movement. Then along came, rolling on the surf, a giant crude-oil spill which devastated San Francisco's precious coastline. I volunteered to rescue oiled birds and got seriously involved in the zoo's wildlife rehabilitation program. In time, armed with my new name, I became the head trainer. Under the direction of Maryrose Spivey, the project's inspired leader, Paul Maxwell, the zoo zoologist and devoted volunteers from the local scout program, we

released many injured, orphaned, and wounded Eagles, hawks, falcons, owls, deer, raccoon, reptiles and worked even with a baby mountain lion. In essence we were teaching Yoga techniques to our animals.

Swami Satchidananda heard of our work and paid a visit to the zoo. I had just extracted from the cage a huge American Bald Eagle named Silver a few days before, and he was in a very dangerous stage of training.

I introduced the Swami to the eagle and the Swami gestured with his arm that he wanted to hold Silver. I protested and refused, explaining the danger, and pointed out the fact that he didn't even have on a glove. The swami insisted!

I had read in many ancient scriptures about holy men who could share their peacefulness with wild beasts. The Hindu Lord Siva, the ancient Celtic Lord Cernnunos, the Lord Buddha, and the Christian Saint Francis. Holding Silver with nothing but a rain cape draped over his arm, the Swami spoke in his deep gentle voice and Silver, now standing close, and looking in his eyes, tucked his wings in a gesture of peace. To a trainer of large and dangerous birds this is a most relieving and sought-after gesture.

When he handed Silver back to me, Silver began his powerful seven-foot wing strokes and tried to fly away with me!

The Swami's demonstration of calm focused determination, coupled with the natural courage which comes from a foundation of deep inner peace, was a profound inspiration to me and my work. This is a potent example of a Yoga Master's ability to transfer his own inner peace to others.

It is a prime goal of Yoga to attain such inner peace and the mastery to share it with others.

It is my goal in offering this book of Hatha Yoga to inspire the reader through examples of beautiful and powerful postures, presented in environments of great power and beauty.

"THE SPIRIT OF UNION'

Deep in the bowels of the Earth are stored,
in capsules, the archives of man.
They tell of a history of great gallantry,
of vast suffering, ignorance and untapped potential.
They tell how in every age and condition
there springs up a breed of unselfish human,
of heroes who answer their nation's last call,
who rise high over walls of hate and stagnation,
living their lives as examples for all,
in "the spirit of union" with time and creation.

The Author, 1981

YOGA
THE SPIRIT OF UNION

Chapter One

Hatha Yoga → Moon-Sun Union.

SUN SALUTATIONS

"The wise cut asunder the Knot of egoism by the sharp sword of meditation. Then dawns the supreme knowledge of self, or full illumination, or self realization. All the bonds of Karma are rent asunder. This is the master key to open the realms of eternal bliss."

Sri Swami Sivananda 1887–1963

The Sun Salutations to follow should be performed in slow, flowing motion. Strive to attain the full extension in each position without over-stretching into the "realms of pain."

NOTES

yoga invented during stone age - technology (5000 years ago) simply - naturally healthy.

"raja - royal" yoga - called "meditation" today.
you are the ruler of your body. Soul is ruler.
"ruler is with itself" - excluding society "meditation"
Body is castle. meditation makes you see you
"royal union" and be "free" from external world.
"silence" - hear thoughts, it tells where the mind is.
yoga, studied 150 years ago by transcendentalists. Meditation to
transcend the mind - travel. Beyond thought. Music changes
the mind by the nature of the sound vibrations
Explore mental capacities not intellectually: through Royal Union.

2

The Tree, Stove Pipe Wells, Death Valley

"Enlighten the people generally and tyranny and oppression of body and mind will vanish like evil spirits at the dawn of day."

Thomas Jefferson 1743–1826: Third president, 1801–1806

"The young lions roar after their prey, and seek their meat from God. The sun ariseth, they gather themselves together, and lay them down in their dens. Man goeth forth into his work and does his labor until the evening."

The Bible: Psalms

Reja royal
Jhana Wisdom
Bhakti spiritual
Karma- lifepath

THE SUN SALUTATIONS (Before beginning, stand as erect as possible with the arms relaxed at the sides; this is called the Mountain Pose.)

1. Exhale to begin the sun salutations, breathing always through the nose, press on the palms.

2. Inhale, lock thumbs and arch back, keeping legs fairly close together.

3. Exhale into a standing forward bend. Keep the legs straight.

NOTES

Body must stay in a union.
Sun is aggressive. Moon is introvert. Muscles heat up as well as cool down. Yoga invented in the stoneage to live longer. 73, 83 life span in Japan. 15 lifespan in the stoneage. Gymnastics, olympics, → Healthy perfection. Barbie Doll syndrome, Miss America syndrome.
Old days did not have image
Asana - positions. let gravity and natural surrounding
Ananda -inner bliss | mastery — animal or man must
master their senses.
Moksha -liberation.   Extend life in tribal society - to become
healthy → next it became as a martial life.
Jhana yoga → as they got older -they got knowlege.
• knowlege   > go to "tribal
elders" to get wisdom→takes grey hair, not like
• wisdom   computers.
Bhakti- search for spiritual union - devotion to higher yoga
Devote to others - other cause. / Bad karma
Karma -deal with past/present &future planting seeds / spreads.
past effects future.

4

Position One—Exhale

Position Two—Inhale

Position Three—Exhale (Point Montara Lighthouse)

COSMIC DRUM

And so I see the universe, all in all as rhythm:
so as with each and every sun heat burst on
*   seashore and globes,*
circling solar systems depths like second-hand clock
*   time,*
sounding changes singly unique with every sentient
*   manifestation.*

The Author, 1977

4. Inhale, lunge one leg far back with knee down and head looking up.

5. Exhale looking under "the mountain," look back at feet and pull heels down.

6. Inhale deeply, lower the knees, chest, and chin and keep the buttocks arched up, like a caterpillar.

Mountain Building

Position Four—Inhale

Position Five—Exhale

Position Six—Inhale

7

'Oh day awake! The atoms' dance
come, in secret I will tell you
where the dance leads us!
All the atoms in the air and the
desert
are charmed like us and whether
happy or sad are stunned by the sun
of the universal soul."

Jelaluddin Rumi 1273 A.D.

7. HOLD the breath as you arch up into the cobra pose.

8. Exhale looking under "the Mountain." Now the sequence begins to repeat.

9. Inhale, lunge the foot up in between the hands, the opposite leg is far back.

The Cobra at Nineteen Months
We all experimented with yoga postures in our youth. At two weeks old Daughter Tara was experimenting with the Cobra, Locust and Boat positions.

Position Seven—Hold Breath

Position Eight—Exhale

Position Nine—Inhale

MOLTEN SEAS

The sun is spotted with seas of molten atoms.
Storms far greater than our own home sphere.
Seas more vast than all our planet brothers.

The Author 1967

10. Exhale into standing forward bend.
11. Inhale into full back bend.
12. Exhale, press in on hands with back erect.

The sun salutations are a comprehensive warm-up even in limited space. Feel free to practice at roadside rest stops, before downhill races or in preparation for important job interviews.

NOTES

September 22

Today I had a disappointing day. I worked on an essay the previous night, to turn in today. Today I also had a test in chemistry class. The test was so long that it ran into my english class. When I got to my english class, my Professor had to remove 10 points from my essay because I came in late. At least I had Yoga afterward so I could relax.

Position Ten—Exhale

Position Eleven—Inhale

Position Twelve—Exhale

"Putting your body in different positions builds strength within the entire system. You tone the muscles, organs, endocrine glands, spine and all the nerve centers.

The asanas (postures) do not cause strain, like many other exercises. They are done very gently with ease and grace."

Sri Swami Satchidananda 1914—

Glacier Point, Yosemite, 8,000 Feet, 1971

Zen in the Art of "Acrophobia Therapy" Annual Squaw Valley Ski Tram Rescue Drill. Leaders: Rob McGir and John Riley, The Dangler: the Author, 1983

"Silence is the most perfect herald of joy"

Shakespeare 1564–1616

Chapter Two

BEGINNING POSTURES

"The most beautiful thing that we can experience is the mysterious. It is the source of all true art and science."

Albert Einstein 1879–1955

The following individual postures are offered in the beginner's sequence. Allow the breath to flow deeply through the nose.

As the postures progress the difficulty increases. The early positions thus prepare and warm the body for the latter ones.

Half Lotus, Borax Canyon, Death Valley

"It is one of the ironies of our time that the techniques of a harsh and repressive system should be able to instill discipline and ardor in its servants—while the blessings of liberty have too often stood for privilege, materialism and a life of ease."

John F. Kennedy, American President, 1961

THE COBRA

"However close we sometimes seem to that dark and final abyss, let no man of peace and freedom despair, for he does not stand alone. If we all can persevere, if we can in every land and office look beyond our own shores and ambitions, then surely the age will dawn in which the strong are just and the weak secure and the peace preserved."

John F. Kennedy 1917–1963

The Cobra can arch to stand erect with the strength and limberness of its spine. This posture warms the entire back, with the focus centered in between the shoulder blades to increase the arch in the upper back. Elbows should be slightly bent.

The mastery of the Cobra begins in our youth

16

Cobra

THE LOCUST

IRON REPTILE

Enter the plains of the San Jouquin
the diesel pumping her reptilian power. It too, the
train slithers, earthbound forever.
Stretching, lean its onward course,
never returning to a land unchanged,
forever enduring the realms of Karma.

The Author 1981

The tree in the second shot is a Jeffrey Pine atop Sentinel Dome, Yosemite. It tells its own tale of the power of Mother Nature's weather cycles and its struggle to survive such power.

The mobile human body can assume many forms to achieve active health. The full locust, shown in its advanced extension is a most dynamic upper back bend. The body weight compresses on neck and chin.

Lie flat, with elbows under stomach and chin forward. Lift legs as high as possible.

NOTES

10/27/2000

Peak Performance is being able to do something in your best condition.

Total Recall is being able to remember fully everything you memorized.

Locust and Train Bridge, Niles Canyon

The Locust and Jeffery Pine, Sentinel Dome, Yosemite

THE BOW

"It was not like taking the veil, no solemn adjuration of the world. I only went out for a walk and finally decided to stay till sundown, for going out I found that I was really going in."

John Muir 1838–1914

The power of a bow is set when the string locks the bow into dynamic tension. In the posture, the arms act as the string—the body, the bow.

A dynamic half circle is thus completed in which the whole being circulates energy. Concentration is on steady and equal tension throughout the entire back, avoiding focused stress in any given area.

The Bow at Four in Fun

Bow

Full Bow—Lake Tahoe

THE FORWARD BEND

"The frontiers are not east or west, north or south, but wherever a man fronts a fact."

Henry David Thoreau 1817–1862

The forward bend is the most simple, yet comprehensive stretch for entire back side, i.e., legs, back and neck.

At first it is done with only one leg out, the opposite leg is folded in with the foot pressed on the inside thigh. Then both legs straight out. Then spread.

No bouncing is necessary—hold steady, breathe deeply, relax into a sustained stretch. For the more limber variation, grab big toes and pull elbows to the ground.

Forward Bend

THE WHEEL

"We know that the original force that created all things is part of the ultimate divinity contained in the universe. Everything living, and inanimate, is part of the whole divine creative force from which it came and to which it flows back. We constantly stress, and it cannot be emphasized too much that it is a major necessity of man, as indeed for all other things, to be in harmony with the environment."

Sybil Leek, a 20th Century Celtic Witch

The most complete back bend is to link the hands with the ankles, thus "the wheel". But first, just arch up the hips, then up on the head, then push up on the arms.

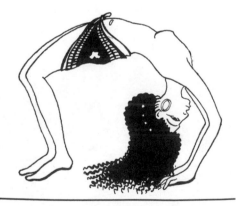

Ancient Egyptian "Acrobatic Dancer" Nineteenth Dynasty, c. 1300 B.C. (Sketched by Beau Caughlan.)

Wheel—Glacier Point, Yosemite, 8,000 Feet, 1971

25

THE SHOULDER STAND AND THE FISH

"Please don't accept something because I said it or because the books say so."

Buddha 500 B.C.

Fish Pose in Full Lotus

The Shoulder Stand

Lift up into the shoulder stand to relieve leg tension. It is a simple inverted pose which stretches the neck, rejuvenates the thyroid, and flushes the brain with good blood.

The Fish

Always perform the fish after the shoulder stand. It's an easy opposite arch and is enhanced with full deep breath through the nose.

For beginners, have the legs straight out on the floor. If you can fold the legs in the full lotus, you can hold the fish in the water, and you will float on the surface like a cork!

Shoulder Stand, Yosemite Falls

27

THE SPINAL TWIST

"If you follow the teaching of one individual, that doesn't mean all should follow him. The one and same spirit expresses itself in many forms and names to suit the age, time, and place. In one place the spirit is called Jesus, in another place, Buddha. There's no need to claim that only one should be worshipped. They are all that one Spirit appearing as different men."

Sri Swami Satchidananda 1914—

To twist is to compress. The whole spinal column is compressed and held steady without the flexing of muscles in this ingenious yoga posture. The arm locked against the leg is the key. The hip and upper back are also participating in a full stretch. The eyes are looking in the direction of the twist.

NOTES

11/10/2000

Today we learned three new yoga positions. They are Throne of shive, Diamond, and Triangle. I also bought a yoga tape. So I can practice at home.

Spinal Twist

THE TRIANGLE

*"Courage is resistance to fear, mastery of fear—
not absence of fear."*

Samuel Clemens (Mark Twain) 1835–1910

This beneficial side stretch is most effective
when done with arms and legs in straight angles.
The eyes stay focused on the raised arm throughout
retention and during the motion in and out of the
posture.

Stretch the arm high over the head when enter-
ing and leaving the triangle. If you bend forward
some at the hips, you will be able to hold the ankle
easily.

Triangle—Sand Dunes, Death Valley

Triangle

THE TRIANGLE (continued)

"Real bliss is maintaining equanimity of mind at all times, at all places, under all circumstances, not only in church or synagogue, but in Times Square or on the battlefield. Closing your eyes and sitting in meditation isn't useful if you become useless as soon as you open your eyes. Yoga is applied equanimity, applied psychology, applied spirituality."

Sri Swami Satchidananda 1914—

An extended variation in the triangle is with the inner leg bent, as demonstrated on the outcrop at Glacier Point.

The Grand Canyon as viewed horizontally in the triangle is none the less awesome.

Triangle—Grand Canyon

Triangle—Glacier Point, Yosemite

THE TREE

"Climb the mountains and get their good tidings. Nature's peace will flow into you as sunshine flows into trees, winds will blow their own freshness into you, and storms their energy . . . while cares will drop off like autumn leaves."

John Muir 1838–1914

A column of steady flowing energy, ever-drawing sunshine, soaking Earth's nourishment, quenching life's thirst.

The posture is one of balanced concentration. The focusing leg is a straight column of energy, extending up into the human trunk. The arms become the limbs. Pressing the palms together over the head raises the center of gravity and increases the sensation of height. To balance thus demands concentration and tunes up the mind.

NOTES

11/17/2000

Today was a do yoga by ourselves day. I felt like I wanted to do yoga longer, but everyone about left and I didn't want to stay forever, plus I had a test to study for. I was glad that I had time to do yoga before a test.

34

Tree, Death Valley

THE DIAMOND

"You will find something more in woods than in books. Trees and stones will teach you that which you can never learn from masters."

Saint Bernard 1091–1153

The diamond is the crystalline form of perfect compactness. The posture is the human form of complete compactness.

Condensed contemplation, relaxed, totally introverted, warm, centered, and the blood flows to the head. A gentle stretch exists in the ankles and knees during the posture.

The question is not how does one climb such a mountain as Castle Peak, but how does one get this Rock up?

Diamond—Alabama Hills, California

AN ODE TO CAT PETER

The Bardo* now hath taken her
From Being into realms beyond
She who taught me Love transcending
That for just Mankind alone.
That Love Was Made For All Of Life:
For Fish that fly through H.2.O. Air;
Birds that Soar beyond Horizons;
Giant Redwoods Circling, Still
Eternal Sunlit Meadows.
Love, Four Legged Creatures All:
From Ant to Zebra, Bat to Goat,
Gazell to Panther to Pachyderm.

The Author, 1969

*Bardo, from the ancient Buddhist manuscript *The Tibetan Book of the Dead;* meaning the "transition zones" from life to death to Rebirth, to afterlife and on to Nirvana.

Other similar words like Moksha, or Mukti, or Liberation, or Enlightenment, or Heaven or Valhalla, or the Happy Hunting Ground are ultimately limited Human terms striving to define the unlimited infinite Realms; and how sad it is that so many wars have been waged and so many good lives lost over "DEFINITIONS".

THE CORPSE POSE—DEEP RELAXATION

"Let us have peace."

Ulysses S. Grant 1822–1885

The art of deep relaxation is simple for all, but mastered by few. Once learned, even during times of extreme stress, all tension can be instantly relieved.

Lie flat on the back, palms turned up. Start relaxing the toes, and work all the way to the scalp.

Stonewall Jackson, during the American Civil War, trained his troops to lie flat on their backs every hour for a full ten minutes. He even trained his horse to lie next to him in deep relaxation. His corps gained the reputation "Foot Cavalry" because they could march faster and farther than any other army in the war. Ironically, before the war, as a mild mannered college professor, he single handedly organized a nation wide prayer for peace; then three years later at a crucial battle he was accidentally killed by his own troops.

Chapter Three

ADVANCED VARIATIONS

"With wings as swift as meditation or thoughts of love"

William Shakespeare 1564–1616

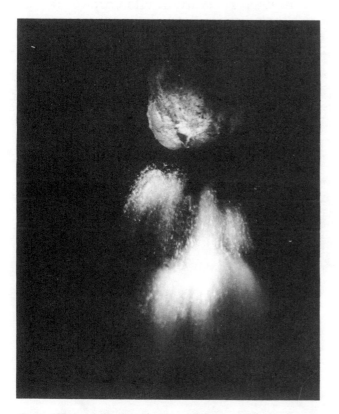

Experiment if you will, but be cautious, for your body has its own limits beyond the command of your mind.

"Body Geography"

Cave Waterfall, Pinnacles National Monument

HAWK EYES

On deep entombed ancient torch
   illumined walls
     Mystic symbols glow
Hand wrought eyes of the Bird of
   Prey
     Gaze out Flame red far below
All seeing wisdom they portray

On high enthroned, a windswept
   Tibetan plateau
     In golden rows towering Buddhas
   pray
Forehead centered third eyes show
     Enlightened vision passed this
   way

On skyward circles, freely soaring
   In fresh high deep blue spirals
The once-god Falcon, master still,
   Scans the pure vast Celtic
   Highland

Here is life's master of speed and
vision whose lightning-bolt eyes
glow, who even now is on the
brink of total extinction. And what
of us humans—without the hawk
of the eye?

The Author 1994

41

THE HEADSTAND

"I am always glad to touch the living rock again, and dip my head in the high mountain sky."

John Muir 1838–1914

Caution!

It's great to view Mother Nature from all angles, but this is outrageous! I NEVER practice yoga in such places. It makes for dynamic photography and may even inspire vertigo, but the actual benefits are lessened because of the extreme danger.

The headstand is the Kingpin of postures—its effects are instantaneous. If the beginner holds it too long at first so is a stiff neck!

Head Stand—Glacier Point, Yosemite

Head Stand, Leg Variation

INVERTED TREE

"Heaven is under our feet as well as over our heads."

Henry David Thoreau 1817–1862

Stand on your head and look up. The Earth is your hat, and your toes mingle with infinity. The inverted tree takes a stronger neck and arms than the headstand. Gravity compresses much energy and blood into the head; an instant mind cleanser. Flip upside down before your next exam or when you are about to fall asleep at the wheel—and wake-up!

NOTES

12/1/2000

Today we learned more intermediate poses. If we could do them, then we are ready to try the next yoga level. We learned about the tree, peacock, head stand, and handstand. most important in yoga is trying to create a strong spine. We also tried more deep relaxation and how to see inward.

Inverted Tree, Death Valley, 282 Feet Below Sea Level

THE SCORPION FROM ELBOW STAND

"Everybody wants to develop their E.S.P. To them I say even with limited sensory perception you are in a lot of trouble. Many things are hidden when you are a child, you are given only a small allowance; as you grow up, it is gradually increased."

Sri Swami Satchidananda 1914—

Once you have mastered the head stand, instead of clasping hands behind the head, place palms down—lower legs into a back bend and lift the head. The balance is then along the forearms and hands. When the back is limber enough, the feet will rest upon the head.

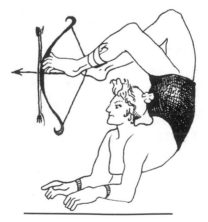

Ancient Roman "Acrobatic Archery" from *Archery* by Dr. Elmer. 1923
(Sketched by Beau Caughlan.)

Scorpion from the Elbows

HORUS THE FALCON OVERLOOKING
THE CROW IN THE LOTUS

*"He opened for me the gates of the heavens; he
threw open for me the portals of his horizon. I flew up
to the sky as a divine falcon in order to see his Divine
mystery in the heavens and adore His Majesty. I saw
the glorious forms of the God of the Double Horizon on
his mysterious paths in the sky."*

Tutmosis III 1504–1450 B.C.

The Crow is a hand balance position. It
strengthens the fingers, wrists, and forearms. In the
lotus, the cross legged lock, the arms are especially
strengthened. The crow can be done out of the lotus,
by simply pressing the knees against the elbows and
pushing up off the toes.

Crow in the Mist, with giant Granite "Crystal." Bridal Veil Falls, Yosemite

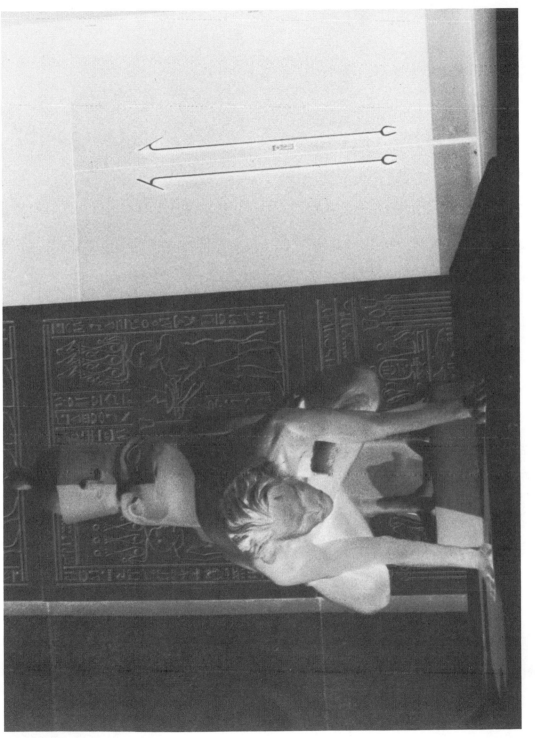

Crow in the Lotus

49

THE UNILATERAL FOOT HAND POSTURE

"Food is from nature, air is from nature, and water is from nature. We take things from nature, so we have to return things to her. We cannot return exactly what we take, but we can convert the food, air, and water into energy for the benefit of the world."

Sri Swami Satchidananda 1914—

Once you have mastered the crow by pushing up on the arms, then set one leg well up over the shoulder, push up on the arms, then lift the extended leg straight.

Unilateral Foot Hand Posture and Lone Pine Peak

THE PEACOCK

"Use no hurtful deceit;
think innocently and justly,
and if you speak,
speak accordingly."

Thomas Jonathan Jackson 1824–1863

Like the noble gait of the peacock who inspires this posture, strive to discipline the body, to hold it straight and horizontal. There comes a noble exhilaration.

A sequence I enjoy is to lower slowly from a handstand, into the full locust, then into the peacock, then back into the full locust, then back into the peacock once again.

Peacock

Peacock—Alabama Hills, CA

THE PIGEON

"I know the stars, the flowers, and the birds
The gray and wintry sides of many glens
And did but half remember human words
In converse with mountains, moores, and fens."

John Millington Synge 1871–1909

The Pigeon is one of the very powerful yoga postures, especially when you can hold the foot with both hands. The pigeon creates a comprehensive stretch in the arms, chest, back and thighs. Because there is a counter pressure in the arm(s) pulling the leg and the leg pulling the arm(s), the posture generates isometric heat or tapas.

Pigeon

Pigeon

THE FULL BOW

"There are some that weigh and measure all in these waste seas.

They that have all the wisdom that is in life, and all that professying images made of dim gold rave out in secret tombs.

They have it that the plans of kings and queens are dust on the moth's wing, that nothing matters but laughter and tears . . . laughter . . . laughter and tears.

That every man should carry his own soul upon his shoulders."

William Butler Yeats 1864–1939

A full circle is completed in the full bow. The legs pull on the arms, the arms on the legs and the body wants to spring to the ground.

"Sequoia," an angry, wild, hungry 7 ft. female American Bald Eagle. (Photo by Greg Estes)

She was captured in British Columbia, Canada and relocated in Big Sur, California. After her release she was shot down in Humbolt County, N. Calif.; later rescued and sent to the San Francisco Zoo with permanent disabilities. One day we hope she will breed. Her offspring to be freed.
(Photo by Greg Estes)

THE WHEEL—EXTENSIONS

"Small waves, big waves, foam, bubbles, spray, and icebergs are one and the same stuff in different forms. A little child welcomes the small waves, a daring fellow who wants to surf ignores the small waves and waits for the big ones. Whichever you choose, see the sea behind them all. Then you will become a seer."

Sri Swami Satchidananda 1914—

Once you can easily press up on both arms in the full wheel, then extend one leg as straight and high as possible. Then one arm, then one arm and one leg! Then one arm and two legs, etc.

Wheel Extensions

Wheel Extensions—Sutro Heights, CA

THE SCORPION, ON THE HANDS

"Inspired by the wisdom of the American Transcendental authors, Thoreau and Emerson, illumined by the crystal clear visionary writings of John Muir and the mystical Bardic poetry of Osian and W. B. Yeats, I embarked on my own quest for truth.

I chose the steep path of the mountaineer and practiced the art of technical rock climbing: The slow motion vertical ballet on Yosemite's awesome granite cliffs. It became for me, my entrance, my gateway and path to the realms of the wild eagle. As I knew that Silver must master his own strength to be free, so I believe that I too must master my own discipline. I practiced the ancient system of Hatha Yoga."

The Author, from an excerpt from
the film "Silver, An American Eagle"

Scorpion

Scorpion
Bad Water, Death Valley 280 ft. below Sea Level with Telescope Peak 11,000 ft.
reflected in the mirage.

THE SCORPION (continued)

"When the ocean comes to one shore it is called the "Pacific". If it comes to another shore it is called "Atlantic" or "Indian". Should we fight and say that the Pacific and Atlantic and Indian oceans have different waters?"

Sri Swami Satchidananda 1914—

I had not intended to perform this posture on such a precarious place as Glacier Point (previous page) but when I got there, the position inspired me. It was only through years of constant Yoga practice and technical rock climbing which familiarized me with extreme heights that there was any semblance of safety. The simple message is that Yoga does nurture self confidence.

The legs can be spread form the scorpion and when lowering forward, hold in an inverted "L" shape.

Scorpion on Hands

Inverted "L" Hand Stand

STRENGTH AND COURAGE—THE KING DANCER

"Our reliance is in the love of liberty which God has planted in us. Our defense is in the spirit which prized liberty as the heritage of all men, in all lands everywhere. Destroy this spirit and you have planted the seeds of despotism at your own doors. Familiarize yourselves with the chains of bondage and you prepare your own limbs to wear them."

Abraham Lincoln 1809–1865

The strength—to hold the posture, the courage—to look skyward, this is especially demanding when, as in the photo, one is atop the 9,114 foot Castle Peak in the High Sierra Mountains. Here the sense of space is pervasive and the focus cannot leave the mind or body.

A Typical 90 Minute Cycle

- Sun Postures, 3 to 7 rounds
- Half and Full Cobra
- Half and Full Lotus
- Bow
- Forward Bends
- Slow Leg Raises, Alternating
- Chin to Knee
- Wheel
- Full Tuck, Knees to Chest
- Shoulder Stand
- Fish Pose
- Spinal Twist
- Diamond
- Triangle
- Tree

Intermediate and Advanced Options

- Crow
- Peacock
- Falcon
- Piegon
- Head Stand
- Scorpion
- King Dancer
- Hand Stand
- Crane

Deep Relaxation

- Eye Exercises; Up-down, Sideways, Circles
- Breathing Exercises
- Deep Meditation

Strength and Courage or King Dancer

LEG TO THE HEAD

"Find me the men on earth who care enough for faith and creed today to seek a barren wilderness for simple liberty to pray."

Helen Hunt Jackson 1831–1886

Children can easily perform this leg stretch. Suppleness is a gift of youth but an investment in old age as well. Contrary to popular belief, advanced Hatha Yoga is not being "double jointed". It is simply youthful limberness maintained. Simple daily stretching reverses the aging, stiffening effects of constant gravity. Gravity in fact is thus transformed into a health-giving force. Each posture is a relationship between the physique and the pull of Mother Earth.

"Freedom, they say, dwells in the hills."

Winston Churchill, *Address*, House of Commons, on the German invasion of Norway, 11 April, 1940.

66

Leg to Head

Leg to Head

THE YOGA SLEEP

"They do not see that they rush towards the abyss. Do not let fools triumph, do not let them throw themselves and us into the abyss."

Grigori Rasputin 1871–1916

Once each leg is limber enough to place behind individually, then lie back to increase the stretch on each. Then place both legs back in the Yoga sleep. Much heat is generated due to compression. Yogis in the high Himalayas can keep warm in this posture. The heat which is generated in many advanced poses is called Tapas.

NOTES

Leg to Head, Lying Back

Yoga Sleep

FIVE BIRDS ROOF PERCHING

BRIGHTENING POWER

Oh to behold the bright
Red-wing blackbird
in the sun
In the spring
In the soul
of my eyes.

The Author, 1981

Sideways Crow

Peacock in the Lotus

The Pigeon is named for its expansive chest.

The Falcon creates a sensation of soaring. The eyes are focused skyward.

The crane, the peacock, and the crow are dynamic handstand variations—and generate much Tapas. As ore is purified by intense heat into pure gold, so Tapas will burn out all the impurities of the human body.

Pigeon

Falcon

Crane

The Rabbit, Basically a Kneeling Bow

"Man must evolve for all human conflict a method which rejects revenge, aggression, and retaliation. The foundation of such a method is love."

Dr. Martin Luther King 1929–1966

Celta, the Irish Wolf Hound and Dunia, the Russian Wolf Hound

HIGH FASHION

Sometimes I wear the old Celtic Cross to remind me
of the Great Masters teaching,
Sometimes I wear the Egyptian Ankh sign in
remembrance of reverence for Life,
Sometimes I wear the Hindu OM sound to remember
respect for each Soul's own Faith
And sometimes I simply wear nothing to reflect that
we all are the Buddha.

The Author, 1980

Alabama Hills, 10,000 ft. Beneath Mt. Whitney, Ca.

"Those who seek Enlightenment must be careful of their each step. No matter how high one's aspiration may be, it must be attained step by step. The steps of the path to enlightenment must be taken in our everyday life."

Buddha 500 B.C.

This immature male Bald Eagle was discovered wounded on Dillan Beach north of the Golden Gate Bridge, thus his name "Dillan." A friend. (Photo by Carolyn Todd)

"Things done well and with care, exempt themselves from fear."

William Shakespeare 1564–1616

"There is one test which we have a right to apply to the professors of all creeds—the test of conduct."

Theodore Roosevelt
26th President

In the ancient Sanskrit Langauge the word Yoga means Union. In the philosophy of Yoga, it is ignorance which is the foundation of all the negative human qualities, i.e., selfishness, greed, hatred, bigotry, religious dogma, political tyranny, and violence. And it is through the removal of one's own ignorance through self-awareness, discipline, study, good actions, humanitarian work, spiritual evolution, brotherhood and sisterhood that one unifies with the cosmic whole.

Hatha (Moon-Sun) Yoga, the emphasis of this work, is the focus on the physical health. To "make friends" with the universal force of gravity using various physical postures. Raja (Royal) Yoga is the mastery of the mind through meditation techniques; Karma Yoga is the use of one's life work for the betterment of all sentient beings; Bhaki Yoga is the union with God; Jnana Yoga is the liberation of mind through philosophical discourse and study.

Pranayama* is an important energizing system complementary to all the Yoga systems dealing with breath control, breathing exercises, and the charging of "the life battery" or "The Force" through deep breathing exercises.

All these branches of Yoga have been practiced and mastered throughout the World in all cultures by all types of people under different names and systems but always with similar results; the betterment of mankind and the Earth he is custodian of—the coming together in the Spirit of Union.

---

*Prana in the Yoga system is equivalent to Mana in Polynesian, Ankh in ancient Egyptian, Chi in Chinese, Manitu in Northeastern American Indian, or Megin or Hamingja in Viking, and in modern lore "May the Force Be With You."

"I am truly sorry man's dominion has broken nature's social union."

Robert Burns 1759–1796

After 5 yrs in captivity, Silver was set free in the Ruby Lake National Wildlife Refuge, Nevada. He lived there happily for ten months.

"So, the struck Eagle stretched upon the plain,
No more through rolling clouds to soar again,
Viewed his own feather on the fatal dart,
And wing'd the shaft that quivered in his heart."

Byron 1788–1824

"It behooves us as humans blessed with modern education to meditate upon the lessons of history."

The Author

"It is through the harmonious discipline of both mind and body that a man can best honor his family, his country, and his gods."

Ancient Greek Olympic Code

Silver, an American Eagle, demonstrating his "Eagle Yoga" to the author. It was their last conversation as Silver was shot and killed by a hunter a few days later.

GURUS

"There is no profession in this country quite as important as the profession of teacher, ranging from the college president right down to the lowest-paid teacher in any one of our smallest country public schools. There is no other profession so important."

Theodore Roosevelt
1858-1919

In the ancient Sanskrit language Guru has two words inside: "Gu" which means ignorance and "Ru" which means removal.

Each life is blessed with Gurus from parents, to kin, to friends, to teachers, to spiritual guides, etc.

There is even a mantra, or prayer, in yoga for gurus which is chanted during meditation as a gesture of thanks.

I like to remember my 8th grade English teacher Mr. Fitzgerald who not only penetrated my thick skull with the illusive laws of English Grammar but also burst out in class once: "Caughlan, you wear your heart on your sleeve"!

My first employer, Dave Fine, at the San Mateo County Fair. He could guess your weight just by looking at you. If he was off by 4 pounds, either way, I'd pass out a prize. Dave first taught me to closely read the Human form

As a High School freshman my Mother said I could study any musical instrument I chose. I said "Conga Drums"! So every Saturday for over a year I took the train to Drum Land in San Francisco to study Latin American Percussion from real master drummers: Armando Peraza, Mongo Santamaria, and Beyardo Velarde.

I learned to play the flute in high school band from Elmer Ravelli and at College of San Mateo Dick

Crest, Bud Young, and Galen Marshall were my advanced "Music Gurus". In Astronomy Dr. Anderson.

At San Francisco State U. Dr. John Tegnell in Voice who trained me to sing with the San Francisco Symphony under the batons of Igor Stravinsky, Robert Craft and Seiji Ozawa. Dr. Roger Nixon in Composition, Dr. Zones in T. V. Aesthetics. "Math Gurus" Dr. Hopka and Dr. Yale Pratt.

At Mills College in Classical Music of India: Masters Kanai Dutta, Tablas; Nikil Bannerjee, Vocals; T. Ranganathan, Mirdangam; T. Viswanathan, Flute. In Javanese Gamelan Orchestra, Mr. Prawoto, Mr. Omartopo.

I learned Bagpipes in my office on the San Francisco State campus from a former Yoga student and master Bagpiper Ian Kelly. Later Pipes and Drums Gurus: Bob Baker, Bill Driscol, Tom Boyle, Kevin Carr.

Bob Chow and Bert Mancini inspired my path in Olympic Target shooting, Ed Canale and Tom Green in Olympic Archery.

Drill Sergeant Evans taught me survival.

There are even such things as Animal Gurus: Cat Peter was a childhood friend. During my wildlife rehabilitation project at the San Francisco Zoo I was blessed with so many amazing Eagle and Hawk "Gurus": Silver, Jane, Altair, Orphan, Geronimo, Tlaloc, Venus, Natasha, Jeb, Blue Beard, Ishi, Charolette, Thor. Big and Small Cats: Brehan, Rowan, Sashi. Snakes Sixteen ft. And down: Comet, Epona, Tarot, Flash.

In wildlife Rehabilitation: Mac Blair, Morlan Nelson, Doug Morris, Ed Ely, Carter Schleicher, Inspectors Ken and Rose McCloud, Cliff Linquest, Frank Craighead, Max Kruger, Sandy Stadler, Sue Kelly, Dr. Bill Hand, and Dr. Sheila Shannon.

Surfing: All the Charter Members of the North Coast Surfers and the SurfRidder Foundation and

Stan Ross; Sailing: Bob Bergthold and Charles Westbook.

Rock Climbing: Edwin Drummond, Les Wilson, Roger Breedlove, Kim Schmidts, Jim Bridwell, Chuck Pratt, Tom Kimbro, Chuck Sayler, Russ Brown, Bill Bonebrake.

Tattoo: Lyle Tutle, Leo Brereton, and Erno.

Forest Fire Fighting Techniques: Art Jasseau. Journalism, Jack Russel, Rich Price.

In Military and Ancient History: Ed Green, Craig Luther, John Shaffer, David Kashimba, cousin Bill Erlmann, Mark Boese and Jim Stevenot.

And finally Spiritual Gurus: Father Brown Morton, Dr. Clint Ervin, Lama Tharthong Tulku. Swami Deviandanda, and Swami Satchidananda, Logan Dallas, my grandmother Nevada Dunn, and the Floating Lotus Magic Opera Company.

LOCO PRECUSSION

On hearing the lonesome train whistle
blowing on down the line:
    oh to be riding 'em high
    over rickety tracks
    cold wind whipping in my hair
    yea my whole body rocking in
    boxcar rhythms

The Author 1968

Wheel with Moon Bridge—Japanese Tea Garden, San Francisco, 1981

"Know thyself"

Inscribed on the Temple at Delphi

"Freedom is indivisible and when one man is enslaved, all are not free."

John F. Kennedy
American president 1963

As a former fire fighter in California I have had many sobering and awesome experiences in vast forests ablaze. One, called The Marble Cone Fire, burned over 150,000 acres of the Carmel Valley and Big Sur Mts. It was the sound of that fire that burned into my memory. But never have I heard a sound so powerful than that of the Olympic flame whipping in the wind as I ran it swiftly on to the U.S. Olympic Festival in Los Angeles, 1991. (Photo courtesy of Ray Oritz.)

Leg Lunge from Scorpion on the Elbows—Rosicrucian Egyptian
Museum, San Jose, California. Photograph taken by Bill Todd.
Reprinted by permission.

APPENDIX I

"This morning a need for Truth is all that is in my mind buried in ignorance, but no scripture past or present can see my future."

The Author 1970

ATTENTION!

This book may be used upside-down or sideways at will, as well as upright.

CAUTION!

It is nearly impossible to learn Hatha Yoga from books, cassette tapes, or video tapes alone. The pace and sequence of postures is necessarily variable according to that individuals personal limitations, and this can only be judged by a competent teacher.

It is however sometimes helpful when using a yoga book to view the Asanas from the perspective of the practitioner in the book, especially the more intermediate and advanced variations. This helps one to gain insight into the physical dynamics involved.

APPENDIX II

HEADSTAND LUNGE

ROCK AN ROLL SOLDIERS

Rock an Roll soldiers
on a magical mystery tour
we rocked to the beat
of 122 millimeter rockets
rolled to the thunder
of distant air strikes
2000 light years from home
we listened to the stones
while watching free light shows
the picture-taking helicopter
flashing the night sky
trying to catch a smile
from the elusive enemy
miniguns lit our fire
with steady streams of red
from the fangs of cobras
and when the music was over
we could never close
the doors.

David Kashimba, Vietnam Vet
and student of yoga, 1948-

Inverted leg lunges are mastered from the headstand first.

APPENDIX III

The Headstand Leg Lunge in the snow with snowshoes creates energy more instant than Espresso! Castle Peak Basin, Donner Summit, Ca. Photograph taken by Carter Schleicher. Reprinted by permission.

APPENDIX IV

LUNGING SCORPION

HOW DOES THE EAGLE SEE

In high flowing rhythm
searching with windsounds by his side
the eagle can see his prey a full 4 miles away.

The Author, 1970

The leg lunge from the elbow scorpion evolves from the headstand and is much more advanced to hold.

Unlike Olympic gymnastics, modern dance, or other "acrobatic" disciplines which point the toes for aesthetic effect, Hatha Yoga Asanas are strictly for power, toes pointed or not.

INSIGHTS OR POEMS

APPENDIX V

Other than the Crane pose on page 71 the lunge from the elbow scorpion is certainly one of the most difficult Asana to hold.

It's not too important to point the toes since yoga is not an aesthetically based system like dance, ballet, or gymnastics..

Yoga is, however, directly linked historically to the many various Asian martial arts disciplines.

Photograph taken by Bill Todd. Reprinted by permission.

APPENDIX VI

HANDSTAND LUNGE PHASE I

"In this country we are long past the stage of regarding it as any part of the state's duty to enforce a particular religious dogma; and more and more the professors of the different creeds themselves are beginning tacitly to acknowledge that the prime worth of a creed is to be gauged by the standard of conduct it exacts among its followers toward their fellows."

Theodore Roosevelt
1858-1919

Solidify handstand first . . .
Photograph taken by Bill Todd. Reprinted by permission.

APPENDIX VII

PHASE II

"The scent of the rose or the ripening corn, the perfumes wafted by a cool evening breeze; all are lost to the nose now adapted to petrol fumes, the stench of duco-spraying and the suffocating atmosphere of entertainment-halls."

Quote from Yoga Asanas by Swami Sivananda, published by Divine Life Society, Himilayas, India

. . . then lunge
Photograph taken by Bill Todd. Reprinted by permission.

APPENDIX VIII

BIBLIOGRAPHY

I. Yoga Postures and Breathing Exercises

Integral Yoga Hatha by Swami Satchidananda. Publisher: Holt, Rinehart, Winston.

Yoga Asanas by Swami Sivananda. Publisher: The Divine Life Society.

Complete Illustrated Book of Yoga by Swami Vishnudevananda. Publisher: Pocket Books.

Light on Yoga by B. K. S. Iyengar. Publisher: Schochen Books.

Yogasana Vijnana—"The Science of Yoga" by Dihrendra Bramachari. Publisher: Asia Publishing House

The Science of Pranayama by Swami Sivananda. Publisher: The Divine Life Society.

II. General Foundation Works on Meditation and Yoga Philosophy

The Practice of Yoga by Swami Sivananda. Publisher: The Divine Life Society.

Three Pillars of Zen by Kaplean. Publisher: Beacon Press.

Remember—Be Here Now by Lama Foundation. Publisher: Crown.

Foundations of Tibertan Mysticism by Lama Govinda Publisher: Samuel Weiser, NY.

The Tibetan Book of the Dead, edition by W. Y. Evans-Wentz. Publisher: Oxford U. Press.

Secret Oral Teachings of Tibetan Buddhist Sects by Alexandria David Neil.

Raja Yoga by Swami Vivekananda.

Science of Yoga by I. K. Tamni. Publisher: Quest Books.

The Morning of Magicians by J. Berigier and L. Pauwels.

The First Heretic, The Life and Times of Ikhanton by Bratton. Publisher: Beacon Press.

Your Sun Sign as a Spiritual Guide by Swami Kriyananda. Publisher: Ananda Publications.

Mastery of Life—A free booklet available by writing Rosicrucian Park, AMORC, San Jose, California 95191.

The Complete Art of Witchcraft by Sybil Leek, 197 Signet.

Bhagavad Gita

Upanasads

Autobiography of a Yogi by Paramansa Yogananda.

Erotic Spirituality by Elisofon and Alan Watts. Publisher: MacMillan.

The Findhorn Garden by the Findhorn Community. Publisher: Harper and Row.

Beyond Words, by Swami Satchidananda. Publisher: Holt-Rinehart-Winston.

Integral Yoga: Yoga Sutras by Swami Satchidananda. Publisher: Integral Yoga Publications.

Modern Yoga Handbook by Vijay Hasasin. Publisher: Doubleday.

The Holy Bible.

The Fairy Faith in Celtic Lands by W. Y. Evans Wentz.

Yeats and the Heroic Ideal by Alex Zwerdling, Publisher: N.Y. University Press.

Futhark by Edred Thorsson Publisher: Samual Weiser Press

last but not least: Zen in the Art of Archery by Eugen Herrigel Publisher: Vintage Books.

APPENDIX IX

IV. Instructional Tapes

Elevation, Level I Hatha Yoga by Lar Caughlan
Life in the Art of Deep Relaxation by Lar Caughlan

III. Music

Deep Sea Echos by Lar Caughlan
Elevation Music by Lar Caughlan
Nocturnes by Emerald Web.
Ambient Nos. 1, 2, and 3 by Brian Eno
Silence Is the Answer by Deuter
Inside by Paul Horn
Himalayan Garden by Mercury Max
Summerland by Danna and Clement
The Master Musicians of India, by Ravi Shankar and
    Ali Akbar-Kahn
Renaissance of the Celtic Harp, by Alan Stivell
Classical Music by Debussy, Ravel, Wagner, Copland, Delius,
    Holst Vaughn-Williams, Satie
Heaven on Earth, Schakie Roth
Dream Waves, Radiance
Within the Wind, Radhika Miller
Down to the wind, Andreas Vollenweider
last but not least, Touch, by Stephen Longfellow Fiske

APPENDIX X

Author Playing Irish Bagpipes

"Deep peace of the running wave to you.
Deep peace of the flowing air to you.
Deep peace of the quiet earth to you.
Deep peace of the shining stars to you.
Deep peace of the watching shepherds to you.
Deep peace of the son of peace to you."

Old Gaelic Blessing

SKETCHES